ESCAPE
FROM HELL

Randall A. Grier

RGM PUBLICATIONS

Unless otherwise indicated, all scripture quotations in this book are from the King James Version of the Bible.

ISBN: 1-57502-214-1

First Printing 1991 RGM PUBLICATIONS
Second Printing 1996 RGM PUBLICATIONS
Third Printing 2003 RGM PUBLICATIONS
Fourth Printing 2005 RGM PUBLICATIONS

Randall Grier Ministries P.O. Box 160
Midland, GA 31820

Printed in USA by Morris Publishing, Kearney, NE

Dedication

I dedicate this book to my Lord and Saviour Jesus Christ, because without Him I would be a failure!

I also dedicate this book to my loving wife, Patricia, without whose love, support, and encouragement I could not have overcome the many obstacles I have faced since my release from prison!

Acknowledgements

I would like to thank our partners for their prayers and support that made this book a reality.

We appreciate those who assisted us in the publication process and for David Savage who spent weeks typing, editing and praying this book together!

I thank God for Rev. and Mrs. D. H. Grier, my parents, and Rev. and Mrs. J. E. Thornton, my daddy and mother-in-law, who have encouraged and supported me.

I express my gratitude to Dr. and Mrs. Kenneth E. Hagin and Rev. and Mrs. Kenneth W. Hagin because, with the exception of God, I would have never made parole from prison nor be successful today were it not for their ministry and training.

Foreword

It is with pleasure that I write the foreword for this book. I believe beyond a shadow of a doubt that this book will stir Christians to joy and thanksgiving. For those who may be in the same situation as Randy was in at one time, I ask that you read his story with an open mind and find out how you, too, can "Escape from Hell."

I became acquainted with Randy Grier when he enrolled at RHEMA Bible Training Center and as he began to attend RHEMA Bible Church where I am the pastor. Randy immediately got involved in doing whatever he could to serve at RHEMA Bible Church. I don't believe I have ever seen an individual so willing to do anything that was asked of him. Whether or not he received any sort of recognition made no difference to Randy-he just wanted to do anything he could to serve the Saviour who had saved and delivered him.

In the many conversations I had with Randy, I could never talk with him for very long without his mentioning that he just wanted to go out and teach others about the Jesus who had set him free! Since his graduation, I have had the opportunity to observe Randy as his ministry has progressed. He is most definitely proceeding to fulfill the vision that God put in his heart while he was still in prison.

Randy's story is one that has been told time after time in the pages of God's Word and through the ages of history. Over and over again, it is the same: Jesus will set you free! You, too, can "Escape from Hell!"

Rev. Kenneth Hagin, Jr.

Chapter 1

I grew up in a Christian home; my daddy was an Assembly of God minister and both my mother and father were Spirit-filled and loved God. Although I was brought up in a Christian home I rebelled against the Lord at an early age. Because of my parents' prayers, and the prayers of others, my life has changed!

During my youth our church offered opportunities for children to grow in the Lord. One of these was a Summer Bible Camp. My parents would send my sister, two brothers, and me to this camp to be built up spiritually. At this camp, we could be trained and taught in the way of the Lord.

My parents sent me to church camp in Waycross, Georgia, in the Okefenokee Swamp, when I was eleven years old. I remember it vividly because it was the beginning of knowing who God is. Once, while at this church camp, all the youth went to the altar praying and seeking God, but I held on to the last minute. I was gripping the back of the bench so tightly I almost rubbed the bark off because I was under the conviction of the Holy Spirit! I knew God was dealing with me, even at this young age. Eventually, I gave my heart to the Lord. I remember lying flat on my back, praying and dedicating my life to the Lord as the Holy Spirit was upon me. During that time the Lord called me to preach His Gospel. He told me that I was commissioned to go and tell the world He was the Savior.

After returning home from church camp, I started telling everyone, "I am called to be a preacher." Soon after, the devil, whom the Bible says, "goes around as a roaring lion seeking whom he may devour," came along and tempted me to turn my back on the Lord.

I eventually submitted to the devil's temptation and turned my back on the Lord. I was attending church and had been sheltered from drugs and alcohol all my life. I didn't know what that scene was all about, but I got involved with the wrong crowd. I was young, about fifteen years old, when I began fooling around with some guys that were attending my church. They were coming to get out of their parents' house, not to worship God. They would borrow their parents' car and say they were going to church but, in reality, they were coming long enough to be seen and then slip off. These boys were secretly smoking cigarettes and drinking beer.

Soon they had some pills and were smoking an odd smelling cigarette. I didn't know anything about marijuana, but later I discovered that this was what they were smoking. By associating with them, they finally talked me into going off with them. Before I knew it I was smoking cigarettes, drinking beer, and smoking marijuana, which led to deeper involvement with drugs. I'm not proud of it, but I tried everything, attempting to find the pleasure I was told about. I can tell you from experience that drugs and alcohol only lead to a life of misfortune and misery! I can't blame parents, friends, or the devil for what happened in my life. Every individual is responsible for his actions; YOU have the final decision concerning YOUR life!

Chapter 2

At age sixteen, I began my experiences with crime and jail. From ages sixteen to twenty, I went to jail more times than I could count and had a record which read like a newspaper. I wasn't in for major crimes, but for charges such as resisting arrest, disorderly conduct, drugs, and auto theft. Eventually, I went to prison for armed robbery.

During one of my jail terms when I was younger, I mingled with older prisoners who were in jail for robbery. These convicts would intrigue me with stories explaining how easy it was to rob people and get away with the money. They told of their fast cars and all the women they had, because of the money brought by robbery. They talked of the fame, glitter, and glory. It didn't dawn on me until later, that these convicts who were telling me about the fame and glory were sitting in a prison cell just as I was. To view it from the proper prospective, they didn't have much sense at all! I was a bigger fool for listening to the lies these convicts were telling about how easy it was to get away with robbery. They were sentenced to life for the very robberies that they didn't get away with. In essence, they didn't get away with anything! These seeds of thought were implanted in me at an early age and the devil began to inspire me and to cultivate the idea about how easy robbery would be.

The whole world desires something for nothing. However, most of the time, when you receive something for nothing, it's not worth anything.

That's the way it is with lying, cheating and stealing; you may receive something for nothing temporarily, but in the long run you'll pay. Be assured that the debt will come due some day!

My partner, the guy I was running around with, and I ran out of money. (I have actually lived in ditches and eaten from trash cans at times; this was my reward for following the devil.) I was selling drugs, but I began to take more of the drugs than I was selling so I ran out of both money and drugs. I was addicted to drugs and alcohol; this addiction causes you to go to any extremes to satisfy your craving. I had a job, but my job wouldn't support my habit so I began these extra activities to support my habit and survive. The seed which was planted years before concerning robbery and how easy it was to get away with entered my mind. The devil planted a thought about how to rob a store I had been in earlier.

The devil works in one's life like this; the devil painted a pretty picture of how I could go into this store, rob them successfully, and get away quite easily. He told me of all the things I could do with the money, and that was all I could think about. The devil does all he can to get you to follow him and the Bible tells us that he transforms himself into an angel of light. The devil lies to everyone and tells them of what glorious things they can do with him, but the end result is destruction. The devil brings things into your life that will result in heartache and separation from your family. There are many people in prisons today who are separated from their loved ones because of their submission to the devil. They knew better but chose to let the devil use them and give them a plan that was supposed to allow them to have some glitter, fame, and glory. The end result however, is always devastating. The devil entices people with drugs, alcohol, illicit sex or whatever. If you fall into his trap he'll snatch you up and cause you to go into Hell's fire! I should have known better than to listen to Satan. In 2 Corinthians 4:4 we are told "that the god of this world (Satan) has blinded the minds of them which believe not, lest the light of the glorious gospel of Christ, should shine unto them." Jesus called Satan a liar, the father of liars; he will offer anything to keep you from receiving Jesus as your Saviour.

To continue with what was happening; my partner and I decided to rob these people. The devil told us how to get the gun, the getaway car, and carry out the plan. We pulled up at the establishment, normally there was only one, maybe two people there. When we began the robbery we were high on alcohol and barbiturates and when we got in the store there were more people present than we thought. The devil's plan was already falling apart!

The event I remember vividly is that I had a .38 caliber pistol cocked and was about to pull the trigger. I was about to kill this person because they refused to give me the money I demanded. Well, I panicked; I was about to blow this person's brains out over a few measly dollars! I started to throw the gun down and run, but I was afraid these people would jump me and kill me so I continued the robbery. My partner and I tried to snatch the phone off of the wall but it was so well attached that we could not, leaving the phone operational. We rushed out and assumed they got a description of the car and us to the police. We didn't care, though, because we were going to ditch the car anyway. I was flying down the road, shifting gears, following the plan of the devil. We had a pile of money and thought we had it made.

Suddenly, the gas pedal linkage jumped off the carburetor and the car stopped because I couldn't give it any gas. I pulled over to the side of the road and took the breather off the carburetor and saw the linkage was loose. I was trying to fix it, scared to death, when about three quarters of a mile down the road, in the direction we were traveling, came a state trooper car. The lights were flashing, siren blaring and he was going as fast as he could go!

When he got close to us he shouted over his P.A. system, "Halt, you're under arrest!" He was going so fast he went by us while trying to stop. Tires were smoking; I slung the breather in the ditch, hooked the linkage up as best I could and slammed the hood shut. We took off, scared to death, wondering what to do. We couldn't shoot it out with the Highway Patrol! Here we were, flying down the road when the devil's plan fails again, the linkage fell off once more. This time it was stuck so that the car would run about forty miles per hour. I'm no genius at mathematics but it doesn't take an Albert Einstein to figure out that if I am running forty miles per hour and the patrol car is traveling at one hundred forty miles per hour, he is going to catch us in just a minute.

I thought about what we could do; the officer would surely shoot us. I saw a curve up ahead and told my partner, "I'm going to run this car into the big gully in the curve and maybe the officer won't see us."

My partner said, "Man, that will kill us!" But I pointed out we would rather be killed by the curve than by the state patrolman. He agreed!

I got to the curve, thinking the police officer didn't see us, and went into the gully, landing in a bunch of kudzu vines. While approaching the curve, I yelled at my partner to get the gun and the money. I knew his hands were free to handle such matters as I was doing all I could to reach the gully. When we landed at the bottom of the gully, we both jumped out of the car and ran through the woods. The officer saw us go off the road and he stopped on the side of the road shooting buckshot down into the gully. When someone is shooting at you, you can run real fast! We ran probably four or five hundred yards before stopping. My partner and I were breathing as hard as we could. He had run completely out of his shirt and shoes.

We were lying down behind some bushes, hearts beating a hundred beats per minute, knowing we were about to die, and I asked, "Where's the money?"

He said, "I thought you had it."

I asked, "Where's the gun?"

He said, "I thought you had it."

I had told him to get them and now we were lying in the bushes, no money, no gun, and no hope of living! We were the big, bad robbers who followed the devil's plan, and it fell through. We took off through the woods again, and soon we heard some bloodhounds;   they must have gotten our scent from the car.

Chapter 3

The robbery occurred around five o'clock p.m. and now it was getting dark. We saw police helicopters flying over looking for us. We were running through swamps and briars and it had been hours now since the robbery and the police were still chasing us. There was no moon out, and we were running through the bushes and briars when suddenly, I couldn't feel bushes hitting my body anymore. I looked up and right in front of me were two state troopers with shotguns. They knew we were heading this way and had sent a car down the county road to spot us. I had run into the right of way on a county road and was staring at these state troopers. They did not see me so I fell back into the bushes. My partner had already seen them; he had stopped several feet back in the bushes and was wondering what in the world we were going to do.

You may wonder why the state troopers didn't see us. The two troopers were standing talking to one another and also had their police radio so loud over the P.A. system that they couldn't hear us running through the woods. They anticipated us coming that direction because the dogs were running that way. There we were, stuck in the woods and scared to death!

From our descriptions, the police thought I might be involved and they, carrying guns, had gone to my mother's and grandmother's houses looking for me.

My mother and grandmother were praying women and they began praying. My mother prayed, "Oh Father God, protect my son, I know he may have done wrong but don't let him get killed. Just protect his life for I know that you have a purpose for him."

If you have been praying for those loved ones for years, you continue to pray! My mother and daddy, along with others, prayed for me for years. They finally broke the powers of darkness so I could pursue the call of God in my life.

The dogs were coming, we were scared to move, and the state troopers were standing there waiting for us. By now, the dogs were about one hundred yards away and you could see them coming through the woods. We could see lights through the woods alongside the dogs so undoubtedly, the dogs were leashed and the officers would find us when the dogs did. We could see them one hundred yards off, fifty yards off, and then about thirty yards away. I told you about my mother praying before to tell you this. What happened had to be supernatural! I don't know if it was because of my mother's prayers or not, but when we get to Heaven we'll ask God. We were lying in the bushes, the dogs thirty yards away, when suddenly they turned one hundred-eighty degrees and headed back down into the swamps. After the dogs headed that way for about three or four minutes, the officers on the road, assuming we had changed direction, got into their car and drove away. After they drove away, we ran across the road and escaped. We stayed in the woods all night long. The next morning I made it to a pay telephone and called some people that I knew to come get us.

So I started running from this crime. After several states and three or four months later, I thought I might have gotten away with the crime because I had not heard anymore about it. Soon after, I was traveling through the same town and was picked up for another charge. I gave them a false name but they found out my true identity and arrested me for the armed robbery which I committed several months prior. They took me to the county jail and booked me. My lawyer said if I didn't plead guilty they would give me a life sentence because of the severity of the crime. I didn't kill or hurt anybody, thank God, but I scared them badly and there were several witnesses to the crime. As much evil as I had done, I couldn't blame anyone for testifying against me. The lawyer told me that if I pled guilty, he could work out a deal, a plea bargain, with the District Attorney, and get me twelve years. So that is what happened. They sentenced me to twelve years in the State Penitentiary.

Chapter 4

When I got to prison I became involved in other things; drugs, prison wine, which is a type of homemade wine, and pills. During the eight years I was there, I escaped three times. Once when I escaped, I left and returned before they ever knew I had gone!

I was an alcoholic and a drug addict; one day we ran out of drugs and alcohol so I escaped to get some more. They had moved me into a cell with some guys who had construction knowledge. I also, could read blueprints and build things. The prison wanted to use inmates to construct a building. They moved us out of the main prison and over to another place where the security wasn't as tight as in the main facility. Late one night, a friend and I decided to slip down to a beer store we knew of and get everyone something to drink. We were going to try to buy some liquor without the people in the store realizing we were convicts. We got outside and eased to the prison stables where horses were kept for checking the fences, and we saddled a couple of horses to ride. Once again, I was following the devil's plan. We rode through the woods and reached the store, but the place was locked and we didn't know anyone able to unlock it. I had been watching too much television and had seen cowboys standing on a saddle. I was sure I could reach the gable end of the store from my horse's saddle. I stood atop the saddle, kicked the attic vent in and entered the attic. Then I kicked a hole into the sheet rock and ceiling plaster, dropping into the store. I let my partner in through the door; he brought some Kroger sacks and burlap bags which we filled with beer, cigarettes, and cookies. We slung them, like saddlebags, onto the horses and rode back to the place where they were keeping us near the prison. We entered the facility. We had enough beer for everyone to get drunk. Everyone became drunk and the situation was a mess. The devil didn't tell us that all the officers had to do was track the horses from the store, back to us!

That is exactly what occurred. The police officers were called and tracked the horses back to the prison. The officers put the heat on a few of the inmates. They were told they would be punished for the crime if they didn't tell who really did it. They told on my partner and me. The officers arrested us and we were placed in the county jail under the jurisdiction in which the crime was committed. The District Attorney told us if we would plead guilty to this charge, he would give us a year and a day. If we didn't, they would give us the maximum penalty allowed. We pled guilty, but when we went before the judge, he wouldn't go along with the recommendation of the District Attorney due to our records. He told us we had been given too many breaks already.

Just like everyone else in life, I had been given many opportunities to get straight. I never took advantage of these chances and I always wound up in more trouble. When this dilemma occurred, I was only thirty days from release on parole; it was almost certain. The devil works this way, trying to keep your life in a mess.

The judge did not go along with the recommendation of the District Attorney and sentenced us to five years, instead of a year and a day. They charged us with burglary and didn't bother to press the escape charge. They sentenced us to five years. By pleading guilty we were granted an automatic appeal if they didn't go along with the deal. We were given an automatic appeal, but they sent us back to the state prison to await trial.

While there, I had to talk with a psychologist. I volunteered to do so because my life was so messed up and I thought he might help me. I remember asking the psychologist if there was a God. Even then God was dealing with me, but I wasn't sure if there was a God or not. The devil blinded my mind to the fact. The psychologist asked me if I believed in a God and said it was not important if he believed, but if I believed. However, I wanted him to tell me if there was a God or not, but he wouldn't commit one way or the other. I am not saying that all psychologists are like this and I am not against them, psychiatrists, or anyone else. But I was confused and didn't know what was going on. Psychologists were supposed to be educated and able to tell me what was happening. Instead, I was prodded, questioned, and locked in cells. I was beaten and harshly treated, probably deserving a lot of it, but everything they tried to help me with didn't do any good at all. I had no control over my life. I could be released from prison one day and be back in the next. That's the kind of life I lived;   the devil motivated me because I allowed him to.

Chapter 5

After about thirty days they returned me to the county jail because I appealed the burglary charge, a felony. They locked me in the third story of the jail so I couldn't escape. A big metal steel door was the only way in or out. I was in an eight by ten cell with one commode, shower, bed, and a metal, fold-down door through which I was fed. That was where I lived, I couldn't get out. I made friends with the man in charge of the keys, and when no one was around he would come into the cell with me and talk. I gave him money and we became good friends.

I knew if I could get one of those keys from him I could escape, but I didn't know how to do it without causing suspicion. I knew he had two keys but I didn't know if I could talk him out of one. One day I remarked that I needed some exercise. I attempted to convince him to give me a key to my cell, but he stopped me immediately. I continued talking and after a long while I convinced him to let me have a key to my cell. That was a convict's dream; to have a key to your own door! I told him that I wanted the key so that late at night, when no one was around I could put my arm out the trap door, and open my door. This would allow me to get into the hallway and exercise. Afterwards, I would lock myself in the cell. He agreed to this.

Soon, they moved another inmate into my cell

with me; I talked with him about my escape plan. Boy, was he grinning and smiling when I showed him the key. My roommate said that if we could get to the second floor without being seen or shot, he knew of an escape route. The prisoners had cut the bars on a window; from there we could travel a fire escape down to the ground. If we could jump over a high fence we could escape without getting caught. That's what we did.

Late one night we opened the cell door and walked out, locking the door back as if we were inside. For some reason, I suddenly had a good heart and didn't want to steal the key. I had been a crook all my life, yet didn't want to take the jail's key! So after locking the door, I laid the key upon the door ledge. We make it down to the second floor without being seen and onto the fire escape, down to the ground, and over the fence. We were afraid our escape would be discovered at any moment, but as it turned out, no one realized we were gone until three or four hours later.

Outside the fence I tried to straight-wire an old car which was close to the jail. When I touched the starter wire and the battery wire together the battery was dead. The devil's plan still wasn't working! So we jumped up, took off down the road and saw a four wheel drive truck parked near the road. I climbed in to see if I could straight-wire it and guess what, the keys were in the ignition. It pays to take your keys out of your vehicle. We pushed the big, four wheel drive Ford out of the driveway and took off flying down the road.

The truck had a lot of trash in the passenger's floorboard, even though it was a new truck. My partner was searching the trash while I was running along about eighty or ninety miles per hour when he let out a holler, "Whooo!" He had found half of a fifth of whiskey. We were drinking that bottle when he found another fifth, unopened. There we were, right on the devil's pathway. Well, when I took my attention off the road to look at that bottle, that is what the devil uses it for, to get your mind off whatever it is you are doing, I ran the truck into a ditch full of soft sand. That shouldn't have been a problem; this truck had a winch on the front big enough to pull down a tree. I got out to hook the winch cable to a tree when I realized that there wasn't a tree anywhere near the truck. Not only that, but the chassis was sitting flat on the ground and four wheel drive or not, the truck wasn't going to come out of that spot.

We jumped out of the truck, took the whiskey, and ran to a factory down the road where we could steal a car. I was in the parking lot looking for a car when I spotted a brand new one with the keys in the ignition. It was just as if the devil had planned for me to come by. I cranked the car, drove around, picked up my partner, and left without alerting any security. We were driving down the road, believing the police were probably looking for us, when we noticed that the car was almost out of fuel.

We stopped by some logging trucks which had fifty gallon tanks hanging from their sides. I figured they kept gas in these tanks so I crept up beside the trucks and, sure enough, by smelling the lids, we discovered gas in the barrels. We cut a piece of hose and made a siphon; then we filled the car from the barrels. I grabbed a five gallon can from one of the trucks, filled it, and placed it in the trunk of the car. After about twenty miles or so the car began jumping and hopping. I found out later that I had put regular fuel in an unleaded vehicle. I didn't realize the difference at that time, however, and the car finally came to a stop on the side of the road.

By this time, the police had discovered our escape. They found the first car, then the truck, and now they knew about this car's disappearance. They put two and two together and placed an all points bulletin for both the car and us. We didn't know what to do about this car, so we decided that we would walk to a store and call someone to come get us. A deputy sheriff drove by, saw the car abandoned, and eventually saw us in the store. He called in a report and waited for us to come out of the store. When we came out, the officer arrested and took us to a county jail.

Chapter 6

They didn't like me at all because I wouldn't admit who I was. I wouldn't tell them I was Randy Grier or anyone else. You can catch a convict red-handed and he won't admit anything. You can go into prisons today and ask a fellow who is guilty, why he is there and he will tell you he is innocent most of the time. That's the kind of convict I was; I was trying to lie to the police officer and tell them that I wasn't the one who committed the crime. They had my description, and I fit the description, but I wasn't going to admit anything. I made them mad so they put me into the "hole" until someone could identify me.

The "hole" was a concrete block room that didn't have a bed, shower, commode, or anything. It consisted of an opening in the floor used as a toilet; occasionally they would bring a little water to drink. The next morning I decided to make friends with the officers so I wouldn't have to sleep on the floor again. I called the jailer, told him who I was, and he said, "We already knew that, we just put you in here because you were so rowdy." He called me out of the "hole." We started talking and he gave me a cup of coffee.

When he got ready to lock me up again, I asked him not to put me in the "hole" because it was such a bad place. He agreed and put me in a cell called the "bullpen," where they kept the bad prisoners. The "bullpen" was a cell with a catwalk all the way around it so the officers could walk around and keep an eye on the prisoners. It had perhaps twelve or sixteen beds. I thought to myself, "Lord, my life is really in a mess now."

Remember I came from the state prison system to go to court on the burglary case, a felony. I escaped, which was another felony, stole a truck, third felony, and stole another car, a fourth felony. In this particular state, in 1980, they passed a law called the Habitual Offenders Act. If you had a record like mine, they would try you under this special law and give you something like one hundred years for a sentence. In other words, you would never get out of prison. I escaped on April 5, 1981, and knew some inmates who received life without parole for just one escape or stealing tool boxes or something. I figured I would get life without parole for all four felony charges so I wanted to escape!

I started talking to these inmates to see who could be trusted not to tell I was going to escape. I believed I had the confidence of one inmate and told him I wanted to escape. He told me I had come to the wrong place! He said few people had escaped from this jail; however, he told me of a possible way to escape from the cell. He showed me a door on the side of the cell which had two locks, one at the top and one at the bottom. The lock on the bottom was sprung but the guards were not aware of its condition. The inmates had pushed on it before and got it to open about four or five inches. It was possible that I might be able to get through the gap and into the catwalk.   However, once on the catwalk, I would have to go down to the first floor where the officers stayed. It wasn't like the place I had been before, this jail was more difficult to escape from.   However, the Federal Government had made the jail install a door at the end of the catwalk in case of a fire. A problem still existed; there were no steps at the door to access ground level. I would have to jump over a tall, high voltage fence. The fence was higher than the door and after jumping it I would fall from the second floor to the parking lot below. No one could conceive I would survive such an obstacle! But the devil sat on my shoulder and told me that I had nothing to lose. He neglected to tell me that if I failed I would have died and wound up in Hell!

So I asked the fellas to help me escape. I talked them into helping me but none wanted to go with me! After the inmates told me where the woods were located and in which direction to run, we decided to begin at dark. Then there would probably not be any officers around. At sunset, we began to push on the door and managed to get my head through the opening. I slid out but the opening I went through was so tight that much of the skin on my front and back was torn. So here I am scared to death, knowing if an officer happened by I was dead. I ran down the catwalk to the fire escape door. When I opened the door, the first thought I had was rational.   I thought to myself, "My God, this is going to kill me!" I was on the second floor looking at a tall, electrified fence about nine feet from the building which I would have to overcome just to get outside the yard.   I would also have to fall down onto an asphalt parking lot and I just knew that was going to kill me. The devil told me, in that matter of seconds in which these thoughts were coming to me, "Well, what have you got to lose? If it kills you when you jump, you won't have to stay in prison the rest of your life." But what he didn't say was that I would have gone to Hell in my condition!

So I went back down the alley way on the cat walk and told the guys I was going to get a running start. They thought I was crazy! I took off running; I'm not sure if I had P.F. Flyers on or not, but I needed them right then! When I hit the door I pushed out and up with all my might because I knew I had to go up and over the fence. I closed my eyes in flight because I didn't want to see what would happen next! When I decided to open my eyes I was right over the razor sharp electric fence. I barely cleared the fence and then fell two stories. Well the rapture wasn't happening and I was going down; of course, if the rapture had been happening I would have gone down anyway! When I hit the asphalt, I landed so hard the impact injured one of my feet. The pain was so severe I almost passed out! Luckily, my adrenaline was pumping so much because of fear that I was able to jump up and begin running on my injured foot. Some of my bones in that foot have humps on them now because I was afraid to go to a doctor.

I ran to the woods and made it to a creek. My foot was in excruciating pain and sweat was running down my chest. Every time I came to a creek I would stop and soak my foot so the swelling would go down and I could continue running. Later, I found out that I ran fourteen miles across swamps, creeks, and even cow pastures.

I got wet when I passed through creeks and didn't know anything about dampness and electric fences. Once while crossing a pasture I slung my leg across a strand of electric fence. Well, the cows were looking and I was shaking, trying to get loose from the fence! Afterwards I was careful crossing pastures, that I can guarantee!

Man, I was in a mess; an injured foot, wet, and running from the law through an unfamiliar area. Finally, it was pitch dark and my plan was to reach another city or town and steal a car to further my escape. When I finally reached a town, I was in so much pain I couldn't even straight-wire a car. The pain was causing me to become sick to my stomach. I was sweating, cold and scared! I just knew any minute I would be shot. I didn't realize that the police were not aware I was gone; they didn't discover my absence until the next morning (I escaped about six or seven in the evening). I just figured that the police were right behind me all the time.

I saw a pay phone and hid in the bushes a long time waiting to use it. Finally, I went to the pay phone and called the same people to come and get me that I had previously called from the store. They said they had been looking for me for two days and I explained I was picked up and escaped again. You can imagine their surprise! I told them that something was wrong with my foot and someone needed to come get me. They told me it would take hours to reach me so I lay waiting in the bushes beside the road. Several hours later, I'm not sure how long, a car pulled up; I jumped into the back seat and we took off.

Chapter 7

This was my third escape. Now I had five felony charges and I knew I was facing life without parole. I was a desperate individual! I started thinking I would try to do what was right and try to make it living out in free society. I made it fine for awhile, but then got involved in drugs and alcohol again.

I borrowed a big old Cadillac from a guy, got a gun, and was up to no good again. Driving down the road on Interstate 95, I sped passed an unmarked car, the officer hit his siren. I had no license nor anything to prove who I was so I knew the officer was going to take me to jail. I pulled over and allowed him to catch up with me because I knew I couldn't outrun him. When the officer got out of his car and started walking toward me, I took off. The officer shot up in the air and I heard him yelling at me to halt. I took the next exit and flew down a country road.

Soon there were police helicopters and road blocks set up to capture me. Before they could get the road blocks set up, I drove between the cars and escaped. Somehow, one of the officers came out a side road while one was behind me and they tried to trap me. They weren't shooting at me, they were just trying to stop me. I found out that, because I was in a big Cadillac, I could take the curves faster than they could. I planned to get far enough ahead of them so I could ditch the car in a curve and run away. I found out later they chased me for twenty six miles across four counties. They had four different county sheriff departments, police, and state troopers after me along with police helicopters.

I was a desperate man! I went into one real sharp curve, and the last I remember the speedometer was bouncing between one hundred and one hundred-fifteen miles per hour. While in the curve, I realized I was going too fast to maneuver. It was a right-hand curve and the back end of the car was sliding around into it. While trying to correct the car, I overcompensated and the car turned all the way around. Now I was going backwards in the direction I was once going forward in. My front end was facing a patrol car and he was running eighty to ninety miles per hour and I am going backwards one hundred miles per hour! The car slid down into the ditch and sat down in the bottom without hurting me.

Police were everywhere; they were shining flood lights down at me and shouting, "Get out of the car, you're under arrest!"

I was afraid to get out of the car because I was an escaped convict. I had a gun and I just knew they were going to kill me. I decided to shoot it out with them. The old devil will tell you that you are able to get away with anything.

I started thinking. Perhaps someone was praying for me; whatever the cause, I decided not to shoot it out with them.

I put the gun under a sack on the seat and a big old burly policeman walked down to the car and commanded me to get out. I don't know if you have ever kissed a flashlight or not, but I did.   When I got out of the car a flashlight came down right across my nose!

As far as I knew it knocked me out; the next thing I knew I was standing in water or something. It was as if I were standing in water and it was deep enough to squish my toes around in. I heard voices as I stood next to a car, handcuffed. I thought water was in my shoes because rain was sprinkling down. I heard an officer remark that someone had better take me to a hospital before I bled to death. It would have been a just end, probably.

What had happened was the flashlight had broken my nose and blood was running down my shirt, into my britches and filling my shoes. My toes squashed around in the blood. The officers decided, after seeing all the blood, that they had better take me to the hospital in the county.

The doctor took me into the emergency room and began examining me. The officers told him my nose had been broken during an auto accident. He did not know an officer hit me and I didn't volunteer the information either. I didn't want to make them any madder than they were! I figured that after the twenty six miles I had run from them, through four different counties, that I had made them very angry. After the doctor examined my nose, he told the officer that he could not release me into their custody. He thought I might have a concussion and if I were to pass out and die somewhere other than at the hospital, law suits might follow. That statement made the officers angry and they tried to persuade the doctor I was okay, but they eventually had to leave.

The doctor put me in a room. This was right up my alley because the hospital didn't know who I was. I had given them a false name and they had no way of knowing my true identity. Once in the room, I made friends with a nurse and asked if I could place some phone calls. The hospital thought I had been in an accident and didn't know about the car chase. They felt sorry for me and allowed me to call some people I knew and asked them to come help me get out of this mess.

My friends came, but by that time the doctor had released me to the officers and they placed me in the county jail. The police still had not processed me properly so they didn't know my true identity. About that time my friends came and got me out on bond. I got away from that situation, went to court and got it taken care of. Now I was free again, but still on escape from prison.

It seemed as though the police were behind me everywhere, chasing and trying to capture me everywhere I went. Many things happened to me in another state; I got busted for drinking, drugs, and driving. By this time I had acquired three different identifications stating I was three different individuals. I pretended to be one certain individual on one of them so I could pay my bond to get out of jail. I had the money to pay the bond, but they require you to stay in jail a certain number of hours. While I was there the police officers went through my wallet and found my other identifications. They started trying to determine who I really was. They kept my wallet and all my I.D.s but released me on bond. So here I am in a mess! Away from home and anyone who could help me.

C h a p t e r 8

I decided to go home and see my folks. I had run out of money and was at the end of my road, miserable with the life I was living. Being on escape from prison may sound exciting to some, but to me it was like Hell on earth! Every time I saw a police officer I just knew he was going to arrest me. On the highway when one would drive up behind me I just knew that he was going to pull me over. I lived in a state of fear constantly!

I went through terrific emotional and physical trauma while on escape and I really wanted to change my life. I was blinded to the fact that Jesus Christ is Lord and the devil had me trapped. That is why it is necessary for us to pray for those who are lied to by Satan. Through our prayer, we have the power to see people saved by the blood of Jesus Christ. Pray that the Lord will send people to them with His word so they can hear, believe and be saved!

On the way to the house I was careful no one saw me because people in the community knew me. I didn't want my mother in trouble for aiding and abetting a criminal. I didn't want to be seen near my family or anyone else because I didn't want them to get into trouble. I went to my mother's house and crept in thinking that no one would see me or tell on me, but that is exactly what happened. I stayed with my mother trying to get my life together, but one day someone saw me at my mother's house and reported I was there.

About six o'clock the next morning the police pulled into the yard. My mother came into my bedroom and of course, I was instantly awakened! I was alert to any unusual sound and of course it is not normal for someone to be driving into the yard at six o'clock in the morning. So I was alert; my mother told me it was the police and that she couldn't lie. What was she going to do? She was a Christian woman and couldn't lie. I told her to go to the door and let them do whatever they wanted; if they wanted to search the house, let them. I intended to hide somewhere. I didn't know where, but I was going somewhere.

Mother went to the door, opened it and the officer said, "Mrs. Grier, we're here to arrest your son; we have been informed that he is here." She didn't say whether I was in the house or not, she just listened. He told her he didn't have a warrant to search her house, but he would like to come inside and look around. Well, if she hadn't let them in, they would have waited around until someone could bring them a warrant so she just let them come in.

I was running around like a chicken with my head cut off, looking for a place to hide! I couldn't figure out where to hide. The officer started looking in the closets, the chimney, everywhere. My mother, the good Samaritan, was helping him through the house. She didn't know where I was and I was still trying to find a place to hide. Have you ever tried to hide in the oven or stove? I pulled the oven door down and tried to fit inside. But I couldn't fit into such a small area and it had all those oven racks as well. I looked under the sink, into the refrigerator; I don't even know why I considered there, because it was full of mustard, bologna, mayonnaise, bread, and stuff. I didn't know what to do! Finally, I wound up in the part of the house where my mother and daddy's bedroom was. This was the only room of the house they had not searched. I was thinking I could hide in a big sliding closet where my mother kept her clothes, shoes, and probably the ironing board. I thought I could get in there and hide.

Now my daddy hasn't moved, even though the officer was in the house searching for me. A storm could come through and daddy would just say, "Huh," and go back to sleep! Nothing moves my daddy. When I went into the bedroom the hall light hit his eyes and he woke up. He wondered what was going on. I told him the police were after me and he wanted to know what in the world I was going to do. Of course, I didn't know exactly what I would do but simply replied that I was going to hide.

Then I said, "Lay down and go back to sleep!"

He said, "Okay," and went right back asleep, "ZZZZZZZZ!" He was asleep!

The officer and my mother, who didn't know where I was, came into this last room. When I tried to enter the closet the door was stuck. Well, I believed if they heard me trying to open the door I would be caught for sure, so I stood in the middle of the bedroom. I could hear them coming; they were talking and mother was trying to help the officer all she could. I had closed the bedroom door, so she grabbed it, swung it open and flipped on the light. She had a dressing chair right beside the door. I plopped right down in the chair. When the officer walked into the room, he walked right beside me, but his attention was focused on my daddy not on me. You see, my daddy was asleep, and now the officer had awakened him. The officer apologized and explained he was looking for me. Well, he was standing right beside me and I thought he had me! I started to say, "Well, you've got me."

I found out later I was obeying a verse in the Bible which says that we are to be swift to hear and slow to speak. So by keeping my mouth shut I actually obeyed that verse without knowing it! I thought the officer saw me and knew I was there but he didn't even look at me.

Now my mother was going to show him no one was there. So she started to open the door wider when she looked around it and saw me; I thought she was going to fall out. Her mouth flopped open, her eyes bugged out, and her expression was one of shock! Her complexion turned white as cotton and she looked as if to say, "Oh my Lord!" Suddenly, she gained her composure and asked the officer if he would like to look in the basement. They turned around and walked out of the room without the officer ever knowing I was sitting beside his feet!

Chapter 9

Well, that was the beginning of the change in my life. After that, I really began to think about the mess my life was in. I realized that I would never be able to go and live anywhere in peace. I had been on the run now for about eleven months. I was miserable. I owned a truck, so I sold it and bought a van. I had no driver's license so I got a buddy to drive my van out of town so if he were stopped, they wouldn't catch me. My friend drove me out of town and I was about to embark on a journey to Baytown, Texas.

You see, while on escape, I met some people who gave me a key to their place in Baytown. They invited me to come and stay with them anytime I wanted to. So I thought I would go to Baytown, get on a shrimp boat in Galveston, and stay out at sea for about four to six months.

I started for Baytown on Interstate 10. While I was driving, I began to think of the mess my life was in and started squalling and crying like the biggest baby you have ever seen. I had never cried like that in my life. I was sick and tired of my life. For the first time in my life, I really wanted to change (Remember, at age eleven, I was called into the ministry). I don't really remember if I was calling on God or not, but I wanted to do what was right. When I reached Baytown I left almost immediately for Galveston. I still wasn't doing right, for I was drinking and taking drugs even then.   But God's mercy endureth forever!

In Galveston, I was driving down Seawall Boulevard, which runs right down by the ocean. I was headed west when I turned around and headed in the direction of the shrimp boats. The police were there, checking identification, and I could have gotten away.

The Spirit of the Lord spoke to me and said, "My Spirit will not always strive with a man, I called you to preach when you were eleven years old, and if you don't turn your life over to me now, you'll never have another chance." Now I knew God was real, and I was scared! When I went to these officers, I lied to them about who I was and they didn't know the truth. While I was sitting there the Lord spoke to me again. He told me I had better turn my life over to him now, or else I would not have another chance because the devil had laid a trap for me.

I had planned to get on a shrimp boat but I said, "Lord, I've got five felony charges and have been on escape for almost a year and don't want to stay in prison for the rest of my life."

God said to me, "Randy, if you'll turn your life over to me, I will straighten out the mess you've made of your life, and I will give you the ability to do what I called you to do."

With tears in my eyes, I asked the Lord what to do? He told me to give myself up to these police officers and plead guilty to the felony charges.   I thought the Lord must have the wrong guy! I was almost killed trying to escape and now He wanted me to return and plead guilty!   But the Lord told me I would have to come clean with him once and for all.

I knew what "come clean" meant; it meant that I would have to be honest and sincere. So I agreed. I turned myself in to the police officers, who found out on their computer that I did have five felony charges pending. They took me to Galveston County Jail where I stayed for thirty days. I waived my rights of extradition, which means I let them take me back across states lines to the state from which I had escaped. When I got back to Alabama I told the lawyer I was going to plead guilty to every charge. He didn't think there was any hope for me.

In fact, the system sent me back to the prison which held all the life without parolees. This was a maximum security prison and the prison system assumed that, with my record, I would get life without parole. After I had been in this prison for about thirty days some of the inmates started telling me they were sentenced to life without parole for only one escape. I had three escape charges and two car thefts; these guys were telling me I would surely get life without parole. There was one inmate who had life without parole for stealing a tool box, so the situation certainly didn't look good for me!

When I went to court, I had already pled guilty to all five felonies. In my mind, the devil was telling me I was foolish; but inside, the Lord gave me peace. The Bible tells us about the peace of God that passeth all understanding. Inside of me I had a peace I couldn't explain. In my spirit and my heart, I knew something good was going to happen, that our Father God would take care of things. Here I was, in front of a judge, having already pled guilty, awaiting a sentence. The judge asked me if there was anything I wanted to say before being sentenced. I didn't have anything to say but my attorney spoke up and pleaded with the judge not to try me under the Habitual Offender Act. He asked him not to give me one single day for the five felonies I pled guilty to. He requested him to have mercy and allow me to return to prison and serve the remainder of the time which I had left.

This was a miracle for my attorney to even say such a thing to the judge about a guy with a record like mine! The judge, supernaturally, for I know it was the Spirit of God, said, "Son, I'm going along with the recommendation of your attorney." I'm not certain of the exact words he used at the time, but he didn't sentence me to one single day for the felony charges. He gave me time, but it was to run concurrent with the time I already had. In actuality, I didn't receive one single day for the five felony charges I pled guilty to!

Tears ran down my face and I knew God had supernaturally intervened in my life and He was getting my life out of the mess it was in. His grace and His mercy is far beyond our comprehension! We might become angry with someone because they slip and fall into sin and we may give them the cold shoulder. But God never would because His mercy reaches further than our human compassion ever could! We should have compassion on our brothers and sisters in the body of Christ and those outside the body of Christ as well. We must not give those out in the world the cold shoulder, but care and pray for them! When I was out in the world, some of the Christians I ran into would despise and treat me worse than anyone else! This was not just in words, but in the way they looked at me as well. Hatred and hateful looks do not originate from love. These thoughts and expressions are not God. Those Christians which treated me that way pushed me away from God! I thought if their actions were of love and of God then I've got as much as they have. Of course, the devil inspired me to think that way.

But in the courtroom, my attorney was excited, and asked permission to stop the court proceedings right then! He wanted the court clerk to bring the paper work to the courtroom immediately so the judge could sign it before he could change his mind! Some people will say I had a good attorney, which I did, but the good attorney I had was not on this earth, but in Heaven. Jesus Christ is better than Perry Mason, the television attorney, ever thought about being! Jesus on your side will never lose your case! The Spirit of God has been speaking to many of you for years now and it is time for you to give your life to Him!

Chapter 10

After I returned to the state prison system from the court proceedings, no one in the prison system knew that I didn't get life without parole. They sent me back to the life without parole prison and the inmates couldn't believe I didn't get one single day for the felonies. I started witnessing about the miracle God had worked in my life. They all thought I was playing a religious game in order to get out. I told them God had worked a miracle for me and I was going to preach the gospel!

I preached my first sermon right there in prison. The chaplain in the prison got to know me and helped me learn the Word of God. He taught me of God and told me he wanted to see lives changed. I started teaching a Sunday School class and eventually we had an outdoor Preach-a-thon. The chaplain let me preach my first sermon in prison, right there where all the death row and life without parole convicts were held at that time. God miraculously anointed me to preach the Gospel! I was a convict who didn't know much, except that I was called to preach.

Another Christian inmate gave me a book to read. It was called *Redeemed From the Curse of the Law* by Kenneth E. Hagin and talked about the curse of the law as found in the book of Galatians 3:13. It states that we, as Christians, were redeemed from the curse of the law which is spiritual death, poverty, and sickness; to tell you the truth I had never heard of such a thing in my life! I thought the book must be of the devil! I had always been led to believe God put sickness on people to perfect them and if you were well off financially you would surely wind up in Hell! I had a footlocker and I placed the book in my locker. Well, the Lord kept dealing with me to read the book, so I got it and my Bible and attempted to prove the book wrong. I found out every scripture mentioned was in the Bible! It wasn't something a man was saying, but it was the Bible and I simply had never heard it before! As I compared scriptures, I found out Jesus is a healer. He redeemed me from spiritual death, and being born again by His Spirit means you'll never have to die an eternal death. John 3:16 tells us that Jesus came to give us eternal life.

I started preaching these things but the devil got mad! The Word of God tells us when the Word is sown into out hearts, the devil comes immediately to take away the Word. He does this by trials and circumstances in which he tries to make the Word to be a lie. The devil believes God is a liar and that he knows more than God. So the devil tries to get us to believe the way he believes. Well, I acquired a small following of inmates who hadn't heard this before either and they began to believe as I did.

Chapter 11

As I began to preach what the Lord was teaching me, the devil attacked me. I don't know what I had, but every bone ached, I couldn't keep any food in my stomach, and I felt as if I were going to die! This went on for about thirty days and I knew in the Word we are told that by His (Jesus) stripes we are healed! Mark 11:23 says that we can have what we say, as long as it is in line with the Word of God. I continued to believe and confess these scriptures were true and for me! Soon, I began to recognize that the devil was attacking me. Until I began preaching I had no sickness, but as soon as I began preaching, here came the devil. My following began to dwindle because they figured if what I preached was true, then I shouldn't be sick. I didn't know all about the trying of one's faith or anything like that. I knew Jesus came and bore our sickness and infirmities and I was going to believe the Word of God! I claimed hundreds of times a day that by His stripes, I was healed. The Bible tells us that faith comes by hearing so I would say this over and over to myself daily. It seemed like the more I said it, the worse I got; the more I believed it, the worse I felt. I lost many pounds and would sneeze about every thirty seconds or so. I looked like Rudolph the red-nosed reindeer.

So after about thirty days of this, the inmates who were following me left, thinking I didn't know what I was talking about. All left except one; Ted, a guy

who was a life without parolee that came to the Lord
through me, stayed with me through all adversity.
He was gloriously born again, filled with the Holy
Spirit, and is on fire for Jesus, even to this day. God
is using him to change inmates' lives in that prison.
Ted and I were praying together one day. We had
prayer every day at five o'clock in the Chapel. When
we finished praying, I could tell by the way he looked
at me that he wanted to tell me something. Ted had a
look on his face that reminded you of an old, sad,
droopy bulldog and he looked as if he had lost his
best friend.

I felt as if I were dying anyway, and he said,
"Brother Randy. I've stuck with you this far, but that
stuff you've been preaching must not be true. If it is
you wouldn't be in the shape you're in; you look as
if you are dying!"

I looked awful in the natural, but everyday,
hundreds of times a day, I proclaimed, "By the stripes
of Jesus I am healed."

When Ted spoke to me that way, a bolt of anger
shot through me! Holy, righteous indignation I might
call it. I jumped up from the pew and told Ted that he
was a liar and that the devil had told him to tell me
that!

The Word of God is true and I didn't care if anyone
stood with me. The Bible says that Heaven and earth
will pass away but the Word will stand forever. I
believe in this everlasting Word and I believed I was
healed even though my body didn't feel like it! I
stomped out of the chapel and didn't want to speak to
him again, a thought which came from anger of
course. I went down to my dormitory and started

praying in other tongues just as hard and fast as I could.

I was angry with God now, because I believed God and knew I was in faith, but my body wasn't healed. I wanted to hear from God about why it wasn't working. When we get serious with God, He'll get serious with us. The Bible says that if we draw near to Him, He'll draw near to us. The Holy Spirit spoke to me; now I don't know if the Holy Spirit has ever spoken to you, but He spoke to me in a voice that was clear and calm. It has happened to me perhaps only once or twice in seven or eight years of being born again. The Holy Spirit spoke to me as I was praying for my healing! He told me to get up and receive my healing for He had given it unto me. Glory to God, I had heard from God supernaturally, and I jumped upon the bed and sat there a moment, but felt just as bad as before. I couldn't figure it out; what did I have to do next? The scripture came to mind that says faith without works is dead; the Holy Spirit also told me that the next time I had to sneeze, refuse it.

I said, "Lord I can't stop myself from sneezing!"

He said, you must act like you want to, for faith is an act and would activate His power to work in my behalf. Well, about that time those tickling sneezes came on me and I spoke out of my mouth that I refused to sneeze and by Christ's stripes I was healed. I said this two or three times when suddenly, the power of the Holy Spirit came on me and I was instantly, miraculously, healed by the power of God! I discovered healing was from Jesus and is for us today! This doesn't mean that everyone will have the same experience as I did. It does mean healing is for

you if you will believe God's Word and receive your
healing!

Chapter 12

After that, everyone started believing my way again because they saw how His power worked. I stood on His Word, and you can, and will, have to do the same. If you are going to have God's power work in your life, you are going to have to stand on His Word. No matter what it is you claim to be yours, whether it is healing, financial needs, salvation, or whatever. You are going to have to stand on God's Word for it and believe in His Word. You may have to do battle with the devil for it, but just stand on His Word! God wants to give it to you, but you must remember that the devil goes about as a roaring lion, seeking whom he may devour!

I got another book called *How to be Led by the Spirit of God* written by Kenneth E. Hagin and found out God lived inside of me. I made requests to Kenneth Hagin Ministries for books and materials and received everything free of charge. If you can get that book, it will literally change your life! The Apostle Paul said, "Know ye not that ye are the temple of God and the Spirit of God dwells in you." I learned to listen to the Spirit of God and He would lead me and guide me as He will you.

The Lord led me to talk to a guy named La T. Da, who supplied dope for some of the inmates who had drug habits. The Lord wanted me to tell this guy that He loved him. I didn't want to get mixed up with this guy because he was a practicing homosexual, sold drugs, and ran around with a pretty bad crowd. This crowd would kill you if they didn't like you. About once a month someone would be attacked or killed in the prison I was in. I lived in an atmosphere where people fought continuously and were murdered out of anger. But the Lord wanted me to go tell La T. Da that He loved him. So I approached La T. Da and told him God sent me to tell him that He loved him. I didn't know how he would react, but he just hung his head. He told me he had used to serve the Lord but backslid and killed a person in a robbery. I witnessed to him as the Lord led me to and finally, he came to church and sat on the very back pew.

We had a minister from the free world to speak that day, and after the sermon an altar call was given. La T. Da walked, almost ran, down the aisle and as he approached the front of the church I met him there. He had been a murderer, thief, homosexual, drug addict, liar, and cheater but I knew that today God would change him! We grabbed each other and hugged and cried for about ten minutes. He repented and cried out to God, and when I stood back and looked upon his face it shone as the face of an angel! The glory of God shone from him and God saved him from all his unrighteousness. You could see the change in him immediately! He told me then that he would not participate in homosexuality or bring drugs into the prison as long as he lived. He didn't realize the magnitude of that statement; for he was about to give his life for his belief in Jesus Christ!

Soon after, because La T. Da had been supplying drugs, some of the guys, especially one that he had practiced homosexuality with, started to put the heat on him. They told him if he didn't come back to their side they were going to kill him. They told him to leave Jesus alone. La T. Da came to me with these threats on his life. We could not go to the authorities with it because if the other inmates found out, you could be killed in you sleep. Not all inmates are like that and neither are all prisons, but that is why we couldn't go to the authorities. He continued serving the Lord and this group of inmates continued to pressure him as they were inspired by the devil.

La T. Da was born again and he, another guy and myself were praying in the chapel about five o'clock one day. La T. Da decided to go to the dormitory and clean up and get ready for chapel service that night. He was washing his face and cleaning up when his ex-partner in homosexuality came up from behind, never said a word, spun him around by the shoulders, and plunged a knife into his heart. He pulled the knife out and stabbed him again in the neck.

I wasn't in the dormitory, but the guys there said La T. Da turned around and looked at him and said, "Man, I ain't got nothing against you." Then La T. Da turned and walked toward his bunk, falling dead in a pool of blood. Some other Christian brothers ran and grabbed a blanket and threw La T. Da on it, running with him to the prison hospital. I could see outside the chapel and when they passed by I knew they carried La T. Da. I prayed that La T. Da wouldn't die, he would live in the name of Jesus. The Lord spoke to me and told me that La T. Da was born again and I should allow him to come on to Heaven. God said that when I get there La T. Da would be there too!

La T. Da is in Heaven now with Jesus Christ and I know if he was here, he would cheer me on and help me all he could to preach the gospel of Jesus Christ! To bring deliverance to those bound by the powers of darkness! God didn't kill La T. Da, the devil did! La T. Da went so deep into sin that it cost him his life to come out of it. The price of sin is too great for you to pay! Jesus is the answer!

Chapter 13

There was another homosexual in this prison for life without parolees the Lord told me to speak to. His name was Donald and he was wild; he committed homosexuality, sodomy, and gambling. I didn't want to fool with him in the natural. I ministered to him because the Bible states the love of God is shed abroad in our hearts and I let this love flow out of me to him. Even some of the other Christian inmates came to me and said I was giving our church a bad reputation. I would walk with Donald on the yard and talk to him because the Lord told me to. Some of the believers disassociated themselves with me, just as some in the Bible did Jesus, because He spent time with the sinners of the world.

Donald would get into poker games and lose everything he had. In this prison, if you owed someone money and couldn't pay, they would kill you; they didn't care since they were already life without parolees. So I took what money I received and paid his debtors to keep them from killing him. One day Donald got into a fight and was locked up in a different part of the prison. I was actually glad because the Lord had given me a seemingly impossible task in taking care of and ministering to this individual. After sixty or ninety days they brought Donald back to our area, yet I felt no strong desire to minister to him as before.

One day Donald came to the chapel, stood and began to testify. He professed Jesus Christ as his Saviour and the Holy Spirit told me it was true. His face began to shine and I knew that all the times I had told him of Jesus and all the work had paid off!

Shortly thereafter, the devil got stirred up and caused a guy who slept on a bunk below Donald to jump up and stab him seventeen times, a brutal murder. The officer there was a rookie and had never seen anything like this. When the stabbing began, the officer ran approximately an eighth of a mile before they could stop him because he was so terrified of what he had witnessed! The Lord gave me peace about this death and assured me he was in Heaven.

Eventually, after about eighteen months in this prison, I was transferred. The transfer was miraculous in itself! I wasn't supposed to go to the prison where I was transferred, but when I arrived I found out why the Lord had brought me there. This prison had a chaplain that was Spirit-filled and loved the Lord God with all his heart, Chaplain Browder. He began to teach and inspire us and allowed us to have an inmate church.

After awhile, the inmate pastor was transferred and the other inmates elected me as the new inmate pastor. It was God's plan. We started having prayer service everyday at noon when everyone came in from their jobs. Inmates would sacrifice their time to come to prayer service. Nowadays you can't get people to sacrifice anything. This just seems to be the spirit of the age. We would sacrifice our time so we could pray for the prison. We would pray for revival and for the salvation of the convicts. There were some hard convicts there, but every day we would meet and pray for the inmates.

Chapter 14

On April 5, 1984, I was out behind the dormitory praying on my prayer path. It was a place I had worn down in the grass from walking up and down praying to God day after day. Hour after hour I would seek God, fasting, praying, and studying my Bible. Anyway, on that day I turned thirty years old, and I was out there praying at approximately noon, awaiting the other guys so we could go to prayer meeting. Suddenly, the Spirit of God fell on me and I almost fell out! The love of God flowed through me and I began to weep like a baby. It was such a wonderful feeling! The Lord told me He was anointing me for the work He called me to do. I didn't know why in the world the Lord would want me. I figured preachers were a dime a dozen and I was just an ol' prison convict. But the Lord reminded me that many are called but few chosen!

He told me some things which would happen in my future. Some of the things which He said have come to pass and others, I know, will come to pass in my future because it is the Lord's plan and will. I argued that I didn't meet the qualifications for becoming a minister! The Lord told me of 1 Corinthians 1:26-28 which says, "that you see your calling, brethren, how that not many wise men after the flesh, not many mighty, not many noble, are called: but God has chosen the foolish things of the world to confound the wise; and God has chosen the weak things of the world to confound the mighty; and base things of the world, and things which are despised, has God chosen, yes, and things which are not, to bring to nothing things which are." The reason He does these things is in verses 29 and 30 which say, "that no flesh should glory in his presence, but of Him are you in Christ Jesus who has God made unto us wisdom and righteousness, and sanctification, and redemption that according as it is written he that glorieth let him glory in the Lord." Praise God, I did meet the qualifications! I certainly was not wise nor noble, and if anyone was ever foolish, it was I. For the devil had dragged me around and I had allowed myself to get into more things than anyone; I was weak. And I certainly had been despised and debased. I knew I met the qualifications if that was all it took to be called of God!

Suddenly, Rob, a guy I had been witnessing to for about five months came walking around the corner. He had known the Lord previously and was once filled with the Holy Spirit with the evidence of speaking in tongues. He had backslid, and was now practicing sinful habits. At that moment, the Spirit of God told me this man was possessed by a demon spirit! The Spirit of God said He wanted me to cast the demon out of Rob; I thought, "Do what?!" I had read about it in books but I had never actually done it. So I started to walk the yard with Rob and the Lord started showing me the difference between this man's personality and the personality of the spirit which controlled him. I had never had this type of experience before in my life, but the Lord had said He was anointing me for the ministry on this day.

By the way, a demon spirit is just a spiritual personality such as you or I, it just doesn't have a physical body to dwell in. So it gets into a human body so it can manifest itself. That's how the devil gets his work done here on earth. That is why there is homosexuality, murders, crime and perversions of all kinds; it is due to demonic powers on this earth. On the other hand, the Holy Spirit wants to indwell us so He may carry out His will and plan here on this earth. When the Lord lives and abides within us, we do his will which is to preach the Gospel. We also help and love our neighbor, and give offerings to support the Gospel. All these things are to further the kingdom of God.

As I walked with Rob, the Lord showed me these things and I went to the chaplain with the situation. The chaplain had told me previously I could use his office at any time. So I told the chaplain about this demon possessed man and what the Lord wanted me to do. The chaplain told me it was certainly possible for Rob to be possessed. He knew the fellow had once followed Jesus and was now a completely different individual. I left and found two Christian friends to help me cast the devil out of him because this was all new to me. One of these guys was a weight lifter named Dixon; you would have to know this fellow to appreciate him. He was young in the Lord and when these homosexuals would get in his face or do something to him he would just knock them down sometimes! He wasn't fully sanctified if you know what I mean! I chose Dixon to help me because I knew he loved God with all his heart. He just had some rough edges God was helping him straighten out and I believe he has the proper attitude now. I also figured he could probably whip the devil by himself, and I had never done something like this and wanted him to go with me!

The other guy was a good, Spirit-filled Christian and they both went with me and the demon possessed guy into the chaplain's office. The chaplain went outside and left us alone, shutting the door. I turned to Rob and asked him what he wanted the Lord to do for him. A person must want to be free from demon possession or else you can't help them. You can't cast the devil out of someone if they don't want him to leave. Just like you can't make someone get saved if they don't want to get saved. But if they are willing, the name of Jesus and His blood can set them free from the powers of darkness. Rob said he had something in his body making him do things he didn't want to do and he wanted to be free from it. I began to command the spirits the Lord had shown me were in him to come out in the name of Jesus!

Now, it was a beautiful, sunny day, not a cloud in the sky, when suddenly, every light in the prison went out. It was as though someone had thrown the main switch, but no one had. The prison was equipped with a large, diesel powered generator which came on during power outages because the security of the prison depended on electricity. It came on, ran about ten seconds, then went off. It did this about three times and finally quit. Now when the electricity fails, the officers immediately take all the inmates and put them back in their respective dormitories. This is because without power, the fences are down and many of the doors are unlocked; so this power outage would cause us to be separated. I didn't know what to do! All I knew was that the lights were out and only a little light shone through the small window in the chaplain's office. Suddenly, I realized in my spirit that the devil had turned the lights out in the prison! I had never heard of such at that time, but since I have been out I have seen and heard of the devil doing supernatural things to hinder God's children.

Here I am, standing here in the chaplain's office, supposed to be the inmate pastor, supposed to be telling these other guys what is going on, and I don't know what to do next! About that time, the chaplain, being sensitive to the Lord, opened the door and told me that the devil had cut the lights out. He told me to hurry and cast the devil out of Rob. He said he would watch for the officers and keep them off of us until we were finished. We had a great chaplain to do this for us!

I turned to Rob and commanded the demons to come out of him in the name of Jesus Christ! When a person is demon possessed, his spirit is possessed by only one spirit. The spirit can open the door for other spirits to come and abide there, but the possession of the victim's spirit is by only one spirit. A good example is that you own your car, you possess that car. If you choose, you can pick up other riders and allow them to ride with you, but you are still the sole possessor of the car. That is the same way demon possession works. As I began to command the demons to come out of him in the name of Jesus, he began to cry and his countenance changed somewhat. We all thought he was free. So I started to try to get him to receive Jesus as his Saviour but he said he couldn't. All of a sudden, another voice spoke up from within Rob. It said there wasn't enough power in the room to cast him out, and we would have to come back when we got enough power!

I had never seen anything like this and my thoughts were that we should leave! The other two guys were looking to me for guidance. I started to tell them, "Let's get out of here," because I had never heard a devil speak before! But all of a sudden, I found myself saying, "You lying devil, come out of him in the name of Jesus!" The Bible tells us that out of our bellies shall flow rivers of living water. The Holy Spirit told me the devil was lying to me! The voice I spoke with was filled with authority, power, force, and fury, when I commanded the devil to come out of him!

When that happened, Dixon, the weight lifter I had taken in there with me, became anointed with the power of God. He reached over and grabbed Rob by the forehead with his hand, shaking him like a dog would a bone. He picked him up, shook him and said, "Come out of him you devil!" Then he slung him back in the chair, Rob fell over on the chaplain's desk and started growling; our eyes grew big as saucers. The chaplain stuck his head in the door and asked what we were doing? I told him we were casting demons out of this fellow!

He could sense what was happening and said, "Don't let that thing get on ya'll, plead the blood!"

Man, were we pleading the blood: The chaplain ran in and assisted us and Rob vomited up something in the trash can. Many people say that if you don't vomit up something then the devil hasn't come out but that is not true. But when Rob vomited, he changed completely and in a matter of moments had accepted Jesus as his Saviour. Soon thereafter he received the baptism of the Holy Spirit with the evidence of speaking in tongues!

Now, I've dealt with demon possessed people and the devil doesn't ever act the same way twice. There's no cut and dried method of how to cast demons out, you just follow the Spirit of God. I just tell the devil to shut up and come out; I don't look for any manifestation. I just tell the devil to come out of the person and let them go in the name of Jesus!

By now the officers had come to get us so we put our new brother in Christ between us and carried him out of there. The officers thought he was drunk! He was drunk, but on a new wine, Glory to God, which came from Heaven! The Holy Spirit filled him to overflowing and he was now restored into his right relationship with God! Now what I want you to understand is that this guy had once before been born again and knew Jesus as his Saviour. He had once before been filled with the Holy Spirit and spoke in other tongues. He backslid and went back out into the world and the devil had taken over his body. According to the Word of God, all I have said is biblical. The Bible tells us in Matthew 12:43-45 that when an unclean spirit is gone out of a man, it walks through dry places seeking rest, and finding none it comes back to the place it came from and finds it empty, swept, and garnished and it enters into the man and brings seven more spirits more wicked that the first. The worse demon possession cases I have ever dealt with were people who had once been saved and Spirit-filled. Then they turned their backs on Jesus and the devil had taken them over again.

Chapter 15

This incident with Rob started a wave of revival! Remember, we had been praying for revival, and the devil didn't want us to get started. We knew the Bible tells us if any two of us agree in prayer, anything they shall ask shall be done for them by our Father in Heaven. The Lord inspired me to gather all the inmates who believed and instruct them to claim someone's salvation based on the verse in Matthew 18:19. It says that if any two agree as touching, anything they ask shall be done for them. There were seventeen of us in prison who agreed to do this. We met out in the yard one day at approximately noon and wrote the names down so each person would be responsible for an individual's salvation. We would agree together that it would be done and then would write their name down on a sheet of paper and see them come to God. We believed it was going to happen! We prayed, called out each individual's name, claimed the verse in Matthew, and believed in unison. I was the only one praying, but the others would agree by saying amen and yes. We agreed and claimed their salvation.

The Lord inspired me to claim a guy's salvation that I used to run around with before my salvation. I had seen him whip lots of guys and though I didn't know it at the time, I found out later he was demon possessed! I went up to this guy and told him the

Lord had told me to claim his salvation. I told him he was coming to God in the name of Jesus! He looked at me as if I had lost my mind, which I had, for now I had the mind of Christ! I went on about my business and about Thursday or Friday I was sitting on the recreation yard. It was some other guys and myself, singing and praising God, when he approached from about forty yards away and told me he wanted to speak with me. I checked my spirit for I knew something was wrong. He told me that for some reason, he didn't know why, he had been plotting to kill me since the day I had spoken to him. He confessed he really didn't want to, but something inside him was motivating him to kill me. His eyes and facial features started changing and I knew it was the devil. Instead of feeling any fear, however, I commanded the devil to come out of him in the name of Jesus and he took off running!

Soon after, it was time to lock down the prison and we had to go back to our respective dormitories. I asked the boys who had been praying to agree with me to bind the spirit that was trying to get this guy to kill me! The Lord had shown me this was the spirit causing him to say and think the things he did concerning me. We agreed and bound the spirit from hurting either him or me. This is scriptural, for the Bible says in Matthew 16:19 that whatsoever we bind on earth shall be bound in heaven, and whatsoever you loose on earth is loosed in heaven. We just read the Bible and believed it, and if you do the same, it will work for you!

The next day, about noon, I decided to do something about this situation. I got those guys to pray, and I set out to find this guy. Believe me, outside I was shaking, but inside I had the peace of God. I found him and began talking to him when suddenly, the devil manifested himself! He started cursing and saying evil things to me. I called the fellow by name and told him I didn't want to hurt him. He knew me, but it was the devil trying to get him to harm me.

Finally, I got him to go with me to the recreation yard. Out here there was a gun tower with a guard carrying a shotgun and a rifle, just in case someone were to attempt an escape. While we were out there, I called Dixon over to give me a hand, and the rest of the prayer group was about a hundred yards away praying. We didn't want to attract attention because the guards might think we were up to something. We started telling him the Lord could set him free from the powers of darkness! All he had to do was give us permission and we could help him get free. Let me tell you this; this guy, I found out later, had grown up in a Pentecostal church. He had been saved, filled with the Holy Spirit, and spoke in tongues. But he backslid, got into crime, and went to prison.

While we were talking to him, he pulled a razor blade from his pocket, prisoners are supplied with them for shaving, and began to try to cut his own throat! I grabbed his hand, and cried to Dixon, "Get the other hand." Dixon had his eyes closed praying so he was unaware of what was going on. I had learned from experience that when you are dealing with the devil, you keep your eyes open! We got the razor blade from him and he jerked away and literally started choking himself with his own hands! He could hardly breath, he was turning red, and his eyes were bulging from his head. We were wrestling with him and finally broke his grip on his throat. Then he reached his fingers into the corners of his eyes and tried to pluck his eyeballs out! We were in shock; I had never seen anything like it in my life! We finally pinned him down but the tower guard thought we were hurting the guy. So he called into the prison and reported that a fight was going on in the yard.

You see, we were always preaching and getting people to receive the Holy Spirit and they would be speaking in tongues right below the guard towers. So they thought we were all crazy!

Meanwhile, we were commanding the demon to come out of him; he was snarling, spitting, cursing us and Jesus. He told us that he was more powerful than us and, of course, we knew this to be a lie.

We started commanding the devil to come out of him! Suddenly, in my spirit, I perceived that the demon was about to leave him and enter someone else. I looked behind me and there stood two rookie officers that had been sent to handle the situation. They were standing, there, eyes bugged out because they saw this guy didn't even look human.

I told them, "Sirs, I know you don't know what I'm doing, but in the Bible Jesus cast out demons and that is what I am doing." I told them that if they didn't want this demon to come out and get into them, they had better leave! They took off and went to the guard office and told what was happening. The lieutenant came out with several guards and asked what we were doing. I told him we were casting out the devil. He said we must do that under the chaplain's supervision if that is what we were actually doing. So they made us let him up and allow him to go. The man ran off, laughing a peculiar laugh, and we proclaimed that we were going to bring him to Jesus!

Later the afternoon, I was at the chaplain's office and told him I had another man who was demon possessed. He said, "Oh my Lord, who is it?" I told him and he agreed.

I asked for his office and he gave me permission. I got four other brothers who loved God but had never cast out demons. I took Dixon with me and we got the demon possessed guy into the office and asked him if he wanted to be free. He said "Yes, I have something in my body making me do these things and I want it out."

As I spoke to him about how Jesus would set him free, he slid out of the chair and under the chaplain's desk. We pulled him out like you would a dog or cat. We cleaned off the chaplain's desk and laid him on his back upon the desk so he couldn't hurt himself; he was spitting and snarling. We started commanding the devil to come out but nothing happened.

I read at one time that Jesus spoke to the mad man of Gaderra and the devil didn't come out at first. Jesus spoke to the demon in Mark chapter 5 and asked its name. The demon said, "My name is legion, for we are many." When Jesus commanded them to leave, they did.

So I commanded the demon and asked, "What is your name? I command you to tell me your name by the authority of Jesus Christ!" The demon refused, but finally told me his name. I commanded this demon by his name to come out of this body and, come to find out, there were ten demons in this guy's body. Remember, only one possessed, the others were like hitchhikers. We finally got the nine to leave and after an hour and a half, the controlling spirit left also. The man received Jesus as his Saviour. We laid hands on him and he received the baptism of the Holy Spirit. God's power moved mightily in that prison!

I had an instructor in Bible School that said, "If you catch on fire, they'll come to watch you burn." People are out in the world hungry for God. The only way souls will be saved is if we take up our crosses daily, follow Jesus, and we will see these things come to pass. Our inmate church would seat about fifty on the pews. We would fill up the seats and the inmates would stand around the walls just to see what would happen next in our church. We had the gifts of the Spirit in operation and there wasn't any telling what might happen in our services! It was nothing like the majority of lifeless services in today's churches.

The church needs a plan of worship but don't stifle what God may want to do in the service. Many churches today, have locked Jesus out of the church service and said that we are going to do it our own way. We need to pray and seek God until we know what he wants to do and then follow His plan.

Chapter 16

Not long after this incident, I came up for parole in May, 1984. The parole board sent me a letter stating that I would be paroled in the month of NONE. I looked on my calendar and couldn't find a month called NONE! What were they saying? They were saying that I would NEVER be paroled. Furthermore, they said I would be reconsidered for parole in the month of NONE. That meant I was never going to be released on parole. I became angry with God because I had been serving Him for almost two years faithfully. I had been ministering to people, casting out devils, healing the sick, getting people born again, and I was angry with God. I thought I was supposed to automatically get my parole because I was serving God! But I wasn't in faith, believing God would take care of the situation.

I went out into the yard with that letter and started praying. "Father God, your Word says if I pray believing I shall have the desires of my heart and you told me I was supposed to go and preach in different places and many other things, but these people are telling me I'm never getting out of here. I believed, what is happening?"

God stopped me right there and showed me that He didn't put me in prison; I did it myself by following the devil. I had run from God since I was eleven and when I rededicated my life to God I was twenty-six; so all that time I had run from God. Had I obeyed

God, I would never have been in jail. God also told me that even though I was praying He would have me released on parole, I didn't really believe it. In Hebrews 11:6 the Word says, "Without faith, it is impossible to please God, for those who come to Him must believe that He is and that He is the rewarder of those who diligently seek Him." God said, "You're not in faith, you're in hope, and hope only sets the goal, but you need faith in order to get out of here. Now write these scriptures down." I filled three notebook pages with faith filled scriptures.

Jesus told me if I obeyed John 15:7 I would walk out of prison; if I didn't I wouldn't. John 15:7 says, "If you abide in Me and My words abide in you, ask what you will and it shall be done unto you." I started walking the prison yard reading those scriptures out loud to myself. God was teaching me what His Word says. Romans 10:17 says, "Faith cometh by hearing, and hearing by the Word of God." As I began to read God's Word aloud to myself, I heard it with my ears as well as my heart. After about an hour and a half of reading like this my faith grew! I knew that no matter what the parole board said, my Father God was going to give me my parole!

After reading these scriptures, the Lord told me I was ready to pray with faith. According to Mark 11:23, "Whosoever shall say unto this mountain, be removed and cast into the sea and don't doubt in your heart but believe those things which you say, you'll have what you say." I had that scripture in my heart and I commanded the parole denials to be removed in the name of Jesus! They gave me about six reasons why I couldn't be paroled, and every one was true,

true about the old man Randy Grier. That old man had been crucified with Christ and my record was washed in the blood. Praise God, I didn't have a record any more! Jesus Christ had cleaned my slate and I could have faith and favor with my Father God. I commanded the parole denials to be cast into the sea according to Mark 11:23. I said, "Father, I believe that I receive my parole in the name of Jesus Christ and I thank you and believe I have my parole now."

In Matthew 16:19, we find that "whatsoever you bind on earth is bound in Heaven, and whatsoever you loose on earth is loosed in heaven." So I turned around and bound Satan in the name of Jesus to loose my parole and let me go about the work the Lord had for me. In the book of Hebrews it says that angels are sent forth to be ministering spirits for them who are heirs of salvation. I knew that the angels would work for me and on my behalf. I thanked God for sending angels to help me in whatever was necessary to bring my parole about!

I prayed and believed that when my mother would go before the parole board the following Tuesday they would change their minds and reverse their decision. I knew I would get out of prison on parole! Now, please don't put God on a time clock, for that's not what I'm saying. If you put him on a time clock you had better make sure you know the will of God.

I called my mother later on that night. I told her that when she went before the parole board they were going to change their minds and let me out on parole. My good old Pentecostal mother didn't want me to get excited and she wanted me to calm down in case it didn't happen. But I knew it would happen because

I had prayed the prayer of faith! I based what I prayed on what God said, not what the devil wanted me to believe! Very politely, I told her I would call her back next Tuesday evening and would find out some good news; then I hung up!

I went about everyday thanking God, "Hallelujah, thank you God for my parole; the devil is bound."

Tuesday night I called my mother on the phone, and when the operator told her who was calling, she began to cry, I finally calmed her down and she told me that from the way things looked and sounded, I would never be released on parole! Every time she told them something good about me, they would tell her ten things that were bad about me. The sad part is that those things were true, about the old Randy Grier, but not the new.

My heart began to sink, faith started leaking out! Then I remembered the Word said, "What things I desire, when I pray, believe that I receive them and I will have them!" So I told my mother it didn't matter what things looked like over there. I still believed my parole would come to pass. I hung up the phone and went by faith, worshipping the Lord Jesus Christ for the great and mighty things he had done for me that day!

The next day was Wednesday, and I woke up thanking God that I had received my parole the previous day. I praised Him for changing the situation and that I was released on parole. Every time my faith got weak, I would read the scriptures on my papers so my faith would be built up. All day Wednesday and Thursday I praised God, believing that I received my parole the previous Tuesday!

On Friday, roll call for mail found me opening a letter from the parole board. The devil told me the letter was confirming what my mother had said. But I knew he was a LIAR and didn't care what the letter said, I had my parole. I opened the letter and it was dated the Tuesday that my mother went before the parole board. It said, "Randall Grier, we have reconsidered you for release on parole." Glory Be To God! I praised God for working that miracle even in the face of contradictory circumstances!

I believe if I had allowed what my mother told me that Tuesday to affect my faith, I would not have received my parole. I lifted up God's Word and did not listen to man, and God's Word came forth triumphant! The Bible says, "Let God be true, but every man a liar." God's Word was true! Three months later, after being told I would never receive parole, I walked out of prison on August 27, 1984 by a miracle of the Lord Jesus Christ! God's supernatural powers set me free!!

Chapter 17

While in prison, I began to think I would be as Paul and not have a wife. I knew I was called to preach and I didn't have time to date any women! But once when I was praying, the Lord spoke to me. He told me one has to have a special anointing to go without a woman in this life. That had never dawned on me before and I didn't realize it. The Lord also told me I did not have that anointing, so I had better pray for a wife!

So I started praying for a wife; I believed it was done and asked the Lord to let me know when I laid eyes on her. The Bible says, "Whatsoever you desire, when you pray, believe that you receive them and then you shall have them." I wanted my wife to be pretty, born again and filled with the Holy Spirit. Also to have loved the Lord all her life, to have never been married and to be faithful to God. I wanted someone who had been called to the ministry and would be compatible with the Lord Jesus Christ and the things which He had called me to do. I told the Lord to show her to me and I would do the rest; for I knew Proverbs 18:22 states, "He that finds a wife finds a good thing and obtains favor of the Lord." I knew the Lord would lead and guide me but I would be the one to take care of getting married and all that sort of stuff.

I was released on parole August 27, 1984, which

was a Monday. That very night, or perhaps the next, I began to attend church services. I didn't care what kind, as long as they loved Jesus and believed in the blood and the death, burial, and resurrection of the Lord Jesus Christ. I went to several churches, trying to stir up the Spirit because they were about half dead!

On the Saturday after the Monday on which I was released, I was looking through a newspaper for church meeting advertisements and one particular ad jumped out at me. It was about a full gospel church beginning a revival that night with a singing, and continuing through the next week. The Lord spoke to me in a still, small voice and told me to attend that meeting. I went to the church and didn't know anyone there. In fact, I had never been there before in my life. I didn't know why I was there, I was just obeying the Lord. He doesn't always explain things in advance.

I walked in and the church was packed out. They were having a meeting, shouting and praising God! I sat in the only place left to sit, which was on the front pew. There sat a young lady beside me, fairly heavy, but a Pentecostal shouter. When the Spirit fell on her she would shout, pray, dance and sing like you've never seen! I wondered how in the world someone so big could move so fast? Now I know this was wrongful thinking, but while she was praying and worshipping, I was praying too: I was praying, "Lord don't let her fall on me!" She was in the spirit though, because she couldn't have done all she was doing, as big as she was, any other way!

After the service I began to leave; I met the pastor

and spoke to him a moment, met the associate pastor and spoke to him. The associate pastor walked out before me and while walking down the steps of the church, he called to me. Out in the church yard there was a street lamp, and as I looked out toward him, I saw behind him, a girl. When my eyes saw her, the Spirit of the Lord spoke up within me and told me she was the reason I went to that church. She was the girl I was going to marry!

She acted as though I didn't exist, but while talking to the associate pastor, I discovered this was the pastor's daughter. She was beautiful and I knew she must have a boyfriend, be married or something.

I went home and told my mother I had seen the woman I was going to marry. She thought I was crazy; I hadn't been out of prison a week. She wanted to know who the girl was. I told her the girl's name was Patti, and my mother immediately described her to me perfectly. Mother told me how good Patti was and how she had served the Lord all her life, and that Patti wouldn't want to have anything to do with me.

I went into my bedroom and shut the door and began praying. I was only human and was afraid I might have missed it. While praying in other tongues, the Lord reassured me. Soon, I discovered that my mother's best friend and Patti were friends. I got my mother's best friend to talk to Patti about me. After she left Patti's house she called and told me to go back to the church and she would introduce us. We made small talk and I didn't see any lights going off in her or anything like that. I sat with her a couple of times and we went to a well lighted place and talked and had a coke to drink.

One night after church, the pastor and his wife invited me to their house so they could see what kind of fellow was interested in their daughter. We were sitting, having cake, coffee, and talking, when Patti's parents arose and left us in the living room alone. I didn't know what to do; I had never been on a decent date in my life. I didn't know whether to read my Bible, talk in tongues, or what! Finally I decided, well, I would pray.

She was sitting on the couch beside me and I extended my hands, which was an indication for her to reach out so we could pray. I said, "Let's pray." I was going to tell Patricia I was going to marry her and this was going to be the way. I prayed, "Father, you said he that findeth a wife findeth a good thing and obtained favor with the Lord and I thank you for this one!" Her eyes shot wide open but I didn't let her go and continued praying. I didn't know if she would scream for her mother or daddy so I kept on claiming it and praying. After prayer, we didn't discuss what I had prayed concerning a wife. We talked some and I left.

She was thirty-one years old and had never been married. The reason was not that she had no dates; she had men trying to date her constantly. The reason was she dedicated that part of her life to the Lord. About three years before I met her, a Spirit-filled lady told her that her husband to be was in a battle for his life and she needed to pray for him.

Now don't accept so-called words from the Lord from just anyone! Many people have gotten into a terrible mess by accepting a "word" from the Lord given them by others! So, if someone gives you a prophecy of some type, make sure it lines up with what you already know in your heart. They should tell you something to confirm what you already have. Some people try to live their lives and make their decisions based on a, so called, word of prophecy from someone else and that is wrong!

During the time the lady told her this, I was on escape from prison and she started praying for her husband as she had never prayed before. So, by now, at age thirty-one, everyone thought she would was going to be an "old maid." She was ready to receive some benefits from the prayer she had invested in this unseen husband! She even wondered if I had been killed in the battle!

After the way I had prayed with Patti she started seeking the Lord. She wanted to find out if I was the right husband for her or if I as just a nut! The Lord spoke to her during this time of prayer and gave her direction. He said I was the one He had for her and I was the one she was to marry.

On Saturday I went over to Patti's house to take her out to dinner. We were sitting on the living room sofa when I told her to call her mom and dad, because I had something I wanted to tell them. They came into the room and paced the floor because they were sure I was going to say something they might not want to hear!

I didn't know any tactful way to say it so I just said to her parents, "I've asked your daughter to marry me and she has accepted and we would like to have your blessings." Patti didn't say anything so I figured she agreed because I never spoke to her about marriage except for the time I thanked God for her in prayer. Their mouths flopped open and their eyes bugged out as they groped for words to say! They thought Patti had lost her mind and tried every way to make sure she had not. She had been saved since a little girl and lived a Christian life and here she was fixing to marry an ex-convict!

Finally her mother sputtered to a stop and said, "My God, Patti you've been without a man so long you're taking anything that comes along!"

Pattie assured her parents that I was the right one and everything would work out fine. Soon, she and I were married; we had a glorious wedding and have a glorious marriage! We love each other very much!!

Chapter 18

While in prison the Lord told me to go to Rhema Bible Training Center. After my release from prison, marriage to Patti, and proving myself to society for over a year, my wife agreed it was God's will that I attend Bible School and we began the preparations. I was about to sell my car to obtain part of my tuition for Bible School when the Lord spoke to me and told me to give my car to an evangelist. I told God if that was actually His will, Patti would agree. When I turned to ask her about it, she agreed it was the Lord's will and we gave the car away!

Now I was in a position where I had to believe God for my tuition! Upon arrival in Oklahoma, I would get up every day, thanking God that I would pay my tuition in full on registration day! One Sunday afternoon, about two weeks before I needed the tuition, a man, John Davis, called.

I had not seen this man but approximately once in the past ten years or so. He said God woke him the previous night and told him to pay my tuition so I could attend Bible School and he was calling to find out the amount. I dropped the phone and began to shout and rejoice in the Lord!! After regaining my composure, I picked up the phone and told him the miracle story about believing God. Then he began to shout, cry, and praise the Lord because he had heard the voice of God!

Before going to prison, I had dropped out of school, and had very little formal education. In prison I passed the General Educational Development test but was still unprepared for any higher educational experiences. Therefore, while at Bible School I had to believe God so I could pass my courses! The Bible says in James 1:5, "That if any man lack wisdom, let him ask of God that giveth to all men liberally and upbraideth not, and it shall be given him if he ask in faith, nothing wavering."

I went to school every day thanking God I had His wisdom and ability and that I would graduate Bible School with straight A's! Upon graduation, I had completed all courses with straight A's. This was TRULY a miracle of God for me!

Since my graduation from Rhema Bible Training Center I have overcome every obstacle I have met as I travel preaching the wonderful news of Jesus! The Lord will truly work miracles in your life if you will only believe! I PRAISE THE LORD FOR GIVING ME ANOTHER CHANCE AT LIFE, THEN HELPING ME TO LIVE IT!!

In June of 1993, I was granted a full pardon as well as the right to bear arms. This simply means I have been pardoned of all crimes and restored to full citizenship!!

The Lord has truly given me a brand new life!

You have read the miracle story of how I escaped from Hell! I escaped from a lifestyle which brought forth, "Hell on earth," and I escaped from literal, ETERNAL, damnation from the FIRES OF HELL!

You may be one who is facing seemingly hopeless situations, believing there is no way out. Jesus Christ can deliver you from all your hopelessness! He came to bring hope to the hopeless, faith to the faithless and deliverance to those who are bound! You must give yourself over to Christ completely, holding nothing back, trusting completely in Him and cooperating with Him and His will.

The way YOU begin to cooperate with Jesus Christ is to accept Him as your Lord and Saviour. As you pray the following prayer, if you believe with all your heart that Jesus Christ gave His life that you may live, you will begin to experience miraculous changes in your life!

Prayer

Dear Lord Jesus, You said in Romans 10:9, "that if I would confess You as Lord and believe in my heart that God has raised You from the dead, I would be saved." Jesus, I confess You as my Lord and Saviour and I dedicate my life to your service. I believe in my heart that God has raised You from the dead. I thank You for my salvation at this very moment!

Amen!

Scriptures That Will Build Your Faith

2 Chronicles 7:14

Matthew 6:33
Matthew 7:11
Matthew 8:16-17
Matthew 10:32-33
Matthew 16:18-19
Matthew 17:20
Matthew 18:18-20
Matthew 21:21-22
Matthew 28:18-20

Mark 9:23
Mark 11:22-24
Mark 16:15-20

Luke 10:17-20

John 3:16
John 14:12-14
John 15:7
John 16:23-24

Romans 10:8-13

I John 5:4
I John 5:14-15
3 John verse 2